Ruell's Publishing
WORKBOOKS

For every child just beginning to shape letters into words, and for the parents, teachers, and helpers who steady their hand along the way.

Writing is more than practice on a page. It is a doorway into stories, a tool for expression, and a small but sure step toward confidence.

This workbook was made to keep learning light, joyful, and steady. a place for tracing, for progress, and for celebrating the little victories that add up to something big.

Ruell's Publishing grants individual teachers permission to photocopy the reproducible pages in this book for use within a single classroom. Reproduction for an entire school, district, or commercial purposes is prohibited without prior written consent from the publisher.

For questions about rights or permissions, please contact:

Ruell's Publishing
www.ruellspublishing.com

ISBN: 979-8-218-77222-2

Printed in the U.S.A.

LEARN TO WRITE

Fun and Engaging Letter Tracing A-Z

Contents

- **Alphabet tracing practice** – Uppercase and lowercase letters A–Z with guided tracing lines.

- **Early learning connections** – Fun illustrations that match letters with simple, familiar words.

- **Pen control & fine motor skills** – Activities designed to strengthen small hands and improve coordination.

- **Brain booster challenges** – Creative activities that encourage problem-solving and critical thinking.

- **Progress notes pages** – A special section for parents and teachers to track growth.

- **Certificate of completion** – Celebrate your child's success at the end of the workbook!

Ruell's Publishing
WORKBOOKS
www.ruellspublishing.com

LEARN TO WRITE

Fun and Engaging Letter Tracing A-Z

This book belongs to

_____

Apple

Aa

Aa Aa Aa Aa Aa

Aa Aa Aa Aa Aa

Aa Aa Aa Aa Aa

Aa Aa Aa Aa Aa

Aa Aa Aa Aa Aa

Aa Aa Aa Aa Aa

*Bonus brain booster!

How many 'a's are in the word Apple? ____

Trace: B is for Ball

Follow the arrows.

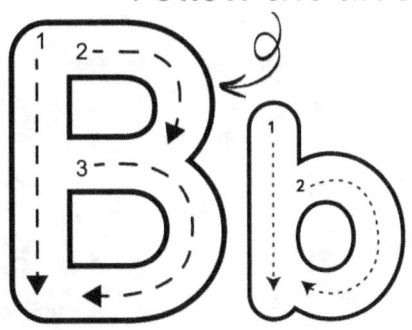

Ball

Bb

Bonus brain booster!

How many 'b's are in the word Ball? ____

Trace: C is for Cat

Follow the arrows.

Cat

Cc

Trace: D is for Dog

Follow the arrows.

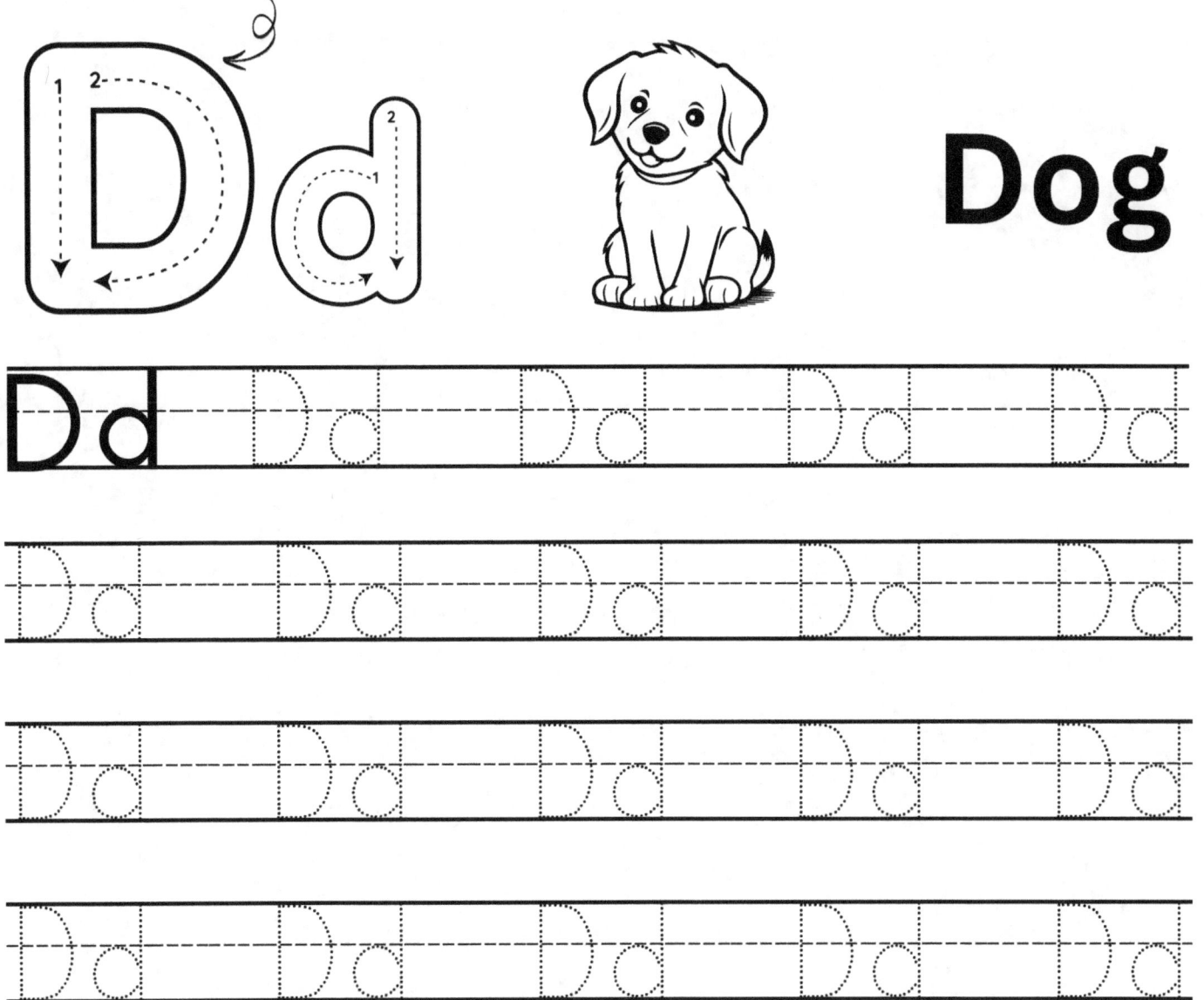

Dog

*Bonus brain booster!

How many 'd's are in the word Dog? ____

Follow the arrows.

E e

Egg

E e

Bonus brain booster!

How many 'e's are in the word Egg? ___

Follow the arrows.

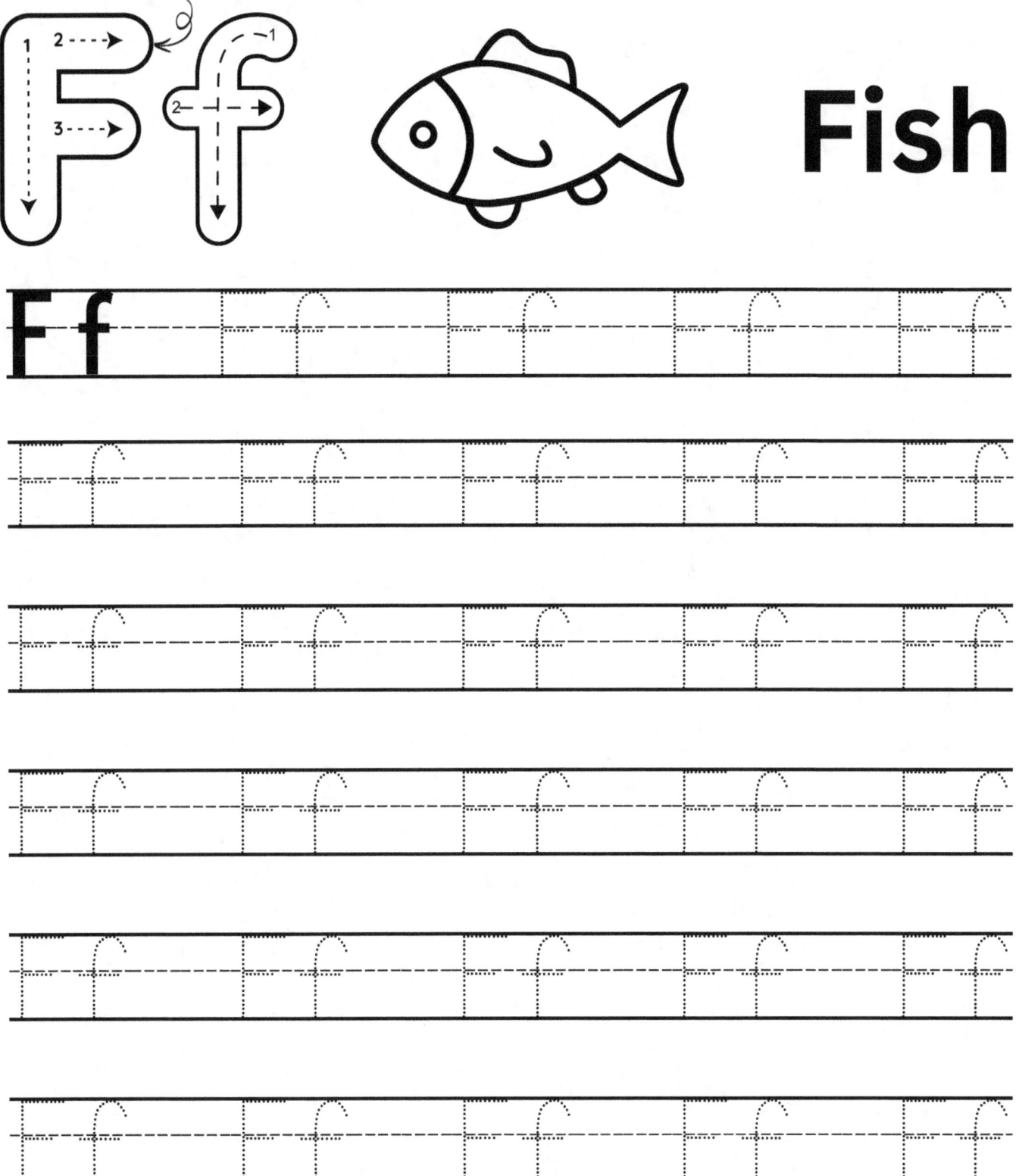

Fish

F f

How many 'f's are in the word Fish? ___

Trace: G is for Goat

Follow the arrows.

Goat

Gg

How many 'g's are in the word Goat? ____

Trace: H is for Hat

Follow the arrows.

Hat

*Bonus brain booster!

How many 'h's are in the word Hat? ___

Follow the arrows.

Igloo

I i

How many 'i's are in the word Igloo? ____

Jam

Jj

Follow the arrows.

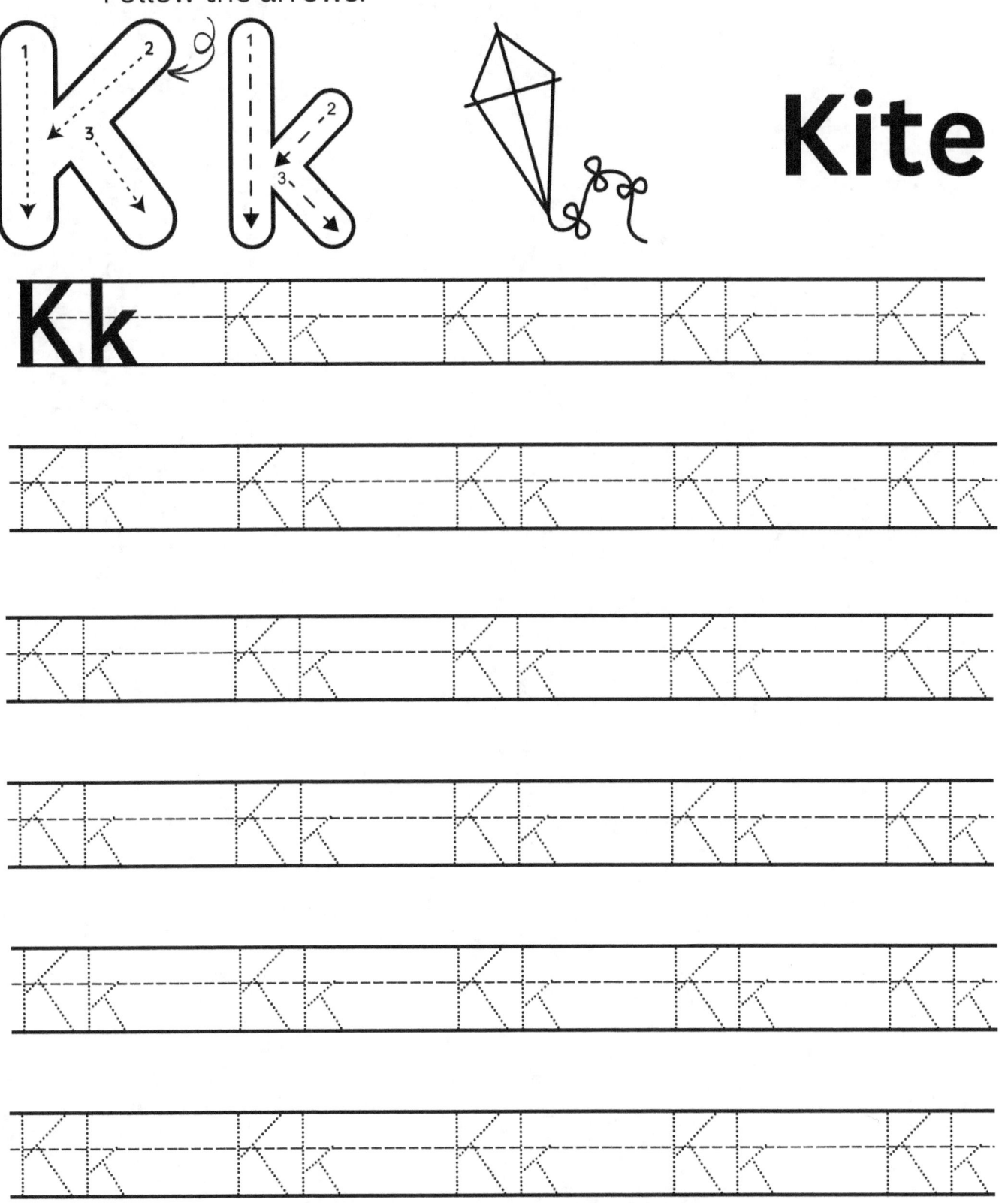

Kite

Bonus brain booster!

How many 'k's are in the word Kite? ____

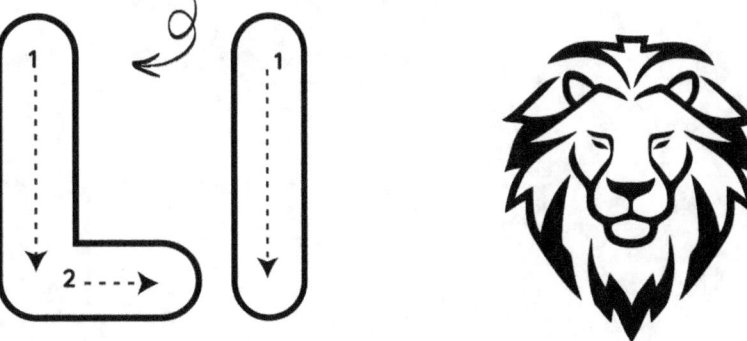

Lion

How many 'l's are in the word Lion? ___

Follow the arrows.

Moon

How many 'm's are in the word Moon? ___

Follow the arrows.

Nest

N n

How many 'n's are in the word Nest? ____

Trace: O is for Owl

Follow the arrows.

Owl

Oo

Bonus brain booster!

How many 'o's are in the word Owl? ____

Trace: P is for Pig

Follow the arrows.

Pig

P p

Bonus brain booster!

How many 'p's are in the word Pig? ____

Queen

Qq

How many 'q's are in the word Queen? ____

Follow the arrows.

R r

Rain

R r

How many 'r's are in the word Rain? ____

Trace: S is for Sun

Follow the arrows.

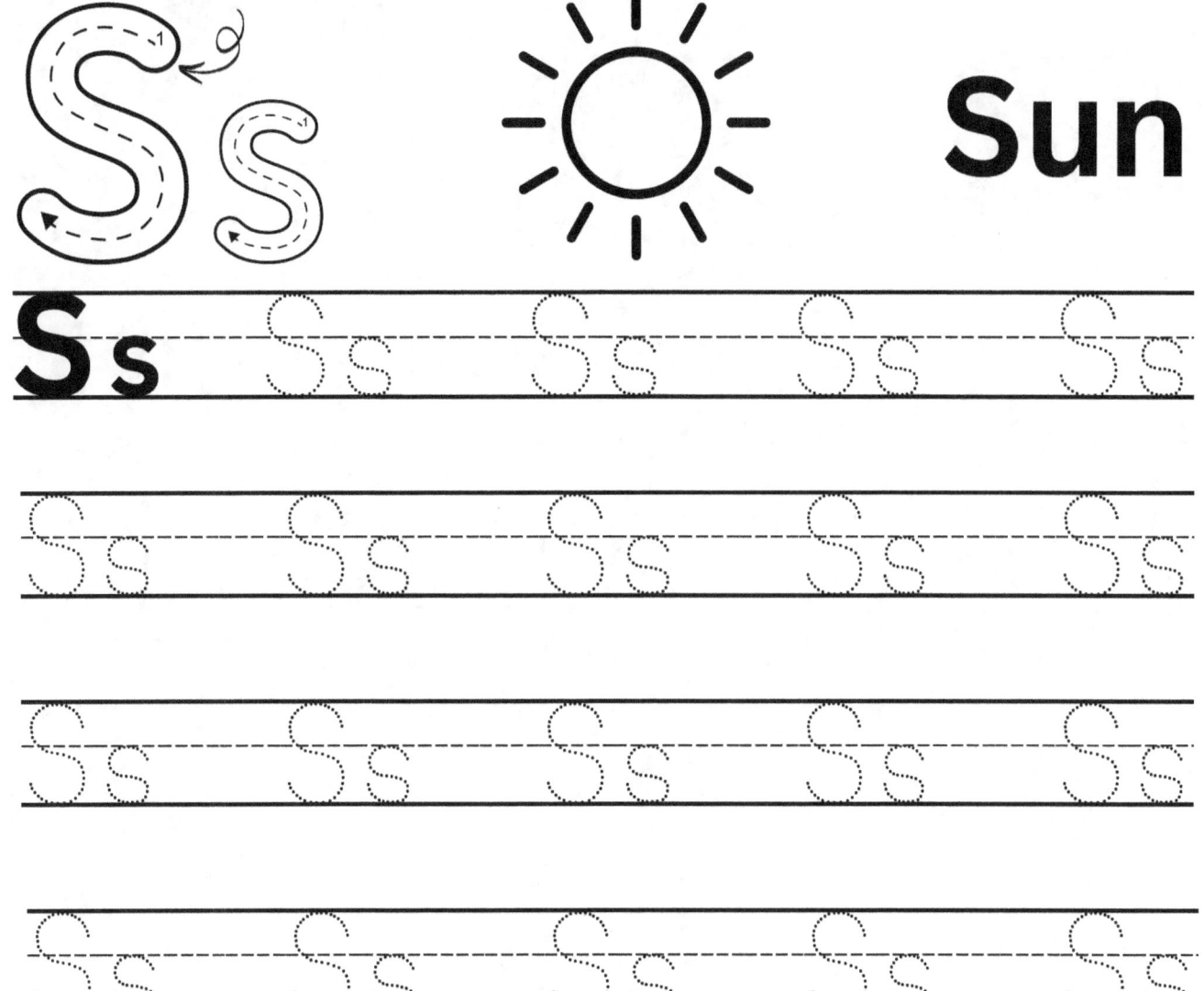

Sun

*Bonus brain booster!

How many 's's are in the word Sun? ____

Trace: T is for Tree

Follow the arrows.

T t

Tree

T t

*Bonus brain booster!

How many 't's are in the word Tree? ____

Trace: U is for Up

Follow the arrows.

How many 'u's are in the word Up? ____

Van

V v

Trace: W is for Whale

Follow the arrows.

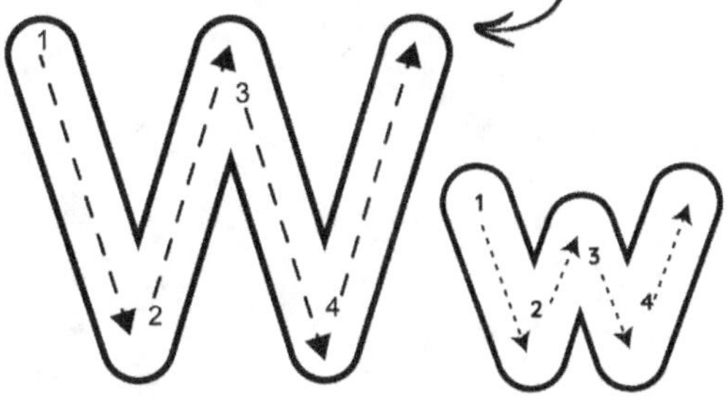

Whale

Ww

***Bonus brain booster!**

How many ‘w’s are in the word Whale? ___

Trace: X is for X-ray

Follow the arrows.

X-ray

*Bonus brain booster!

How many 'x's are in the word X-ray? ___

Trace: Y is for Yak

Follow the arrows.

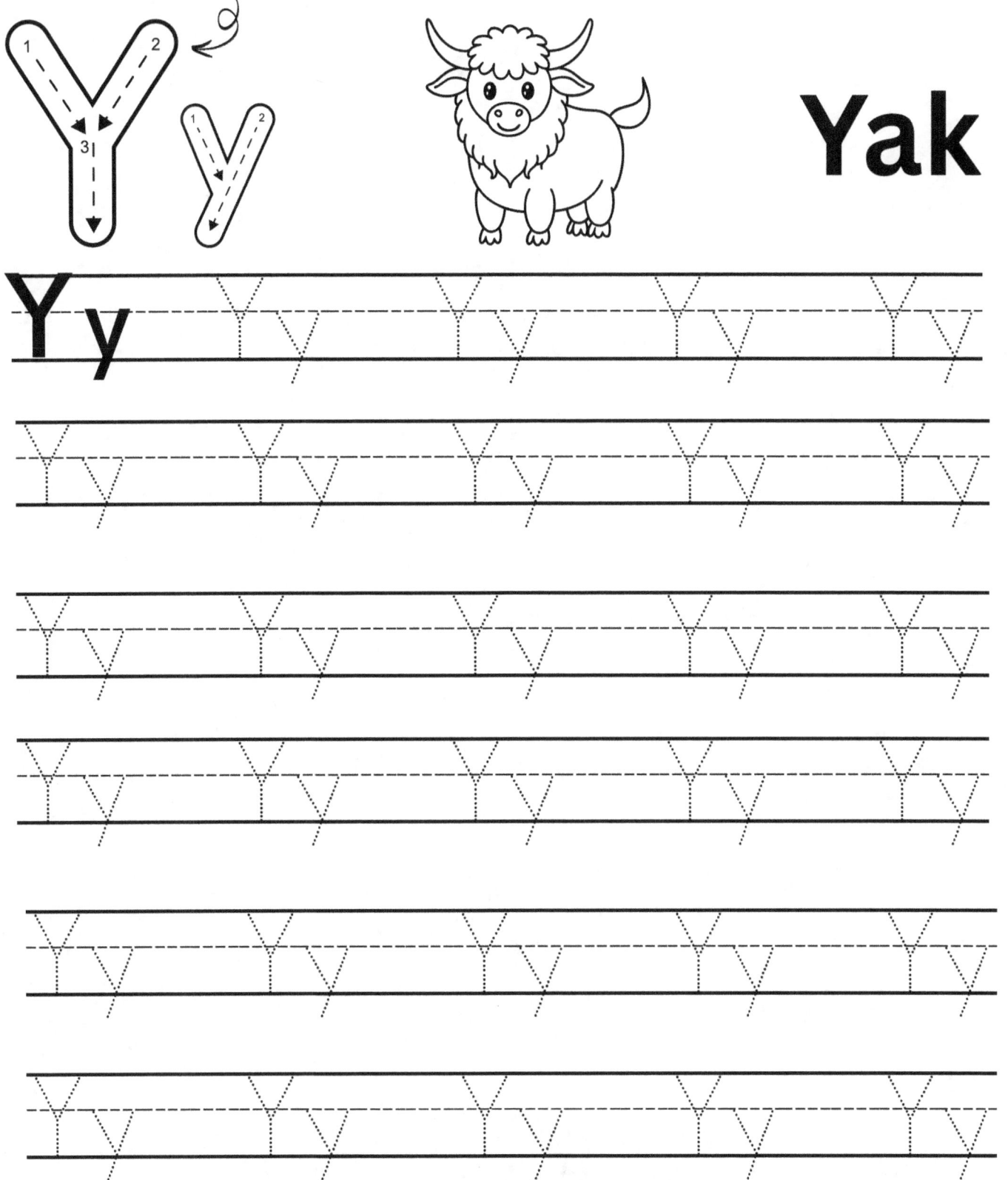

Yak

Yy

*Bonus brain booster!

How many 'y's are in the word Yak? ____

Trace: Z is for Zebra

Follow the arrows.

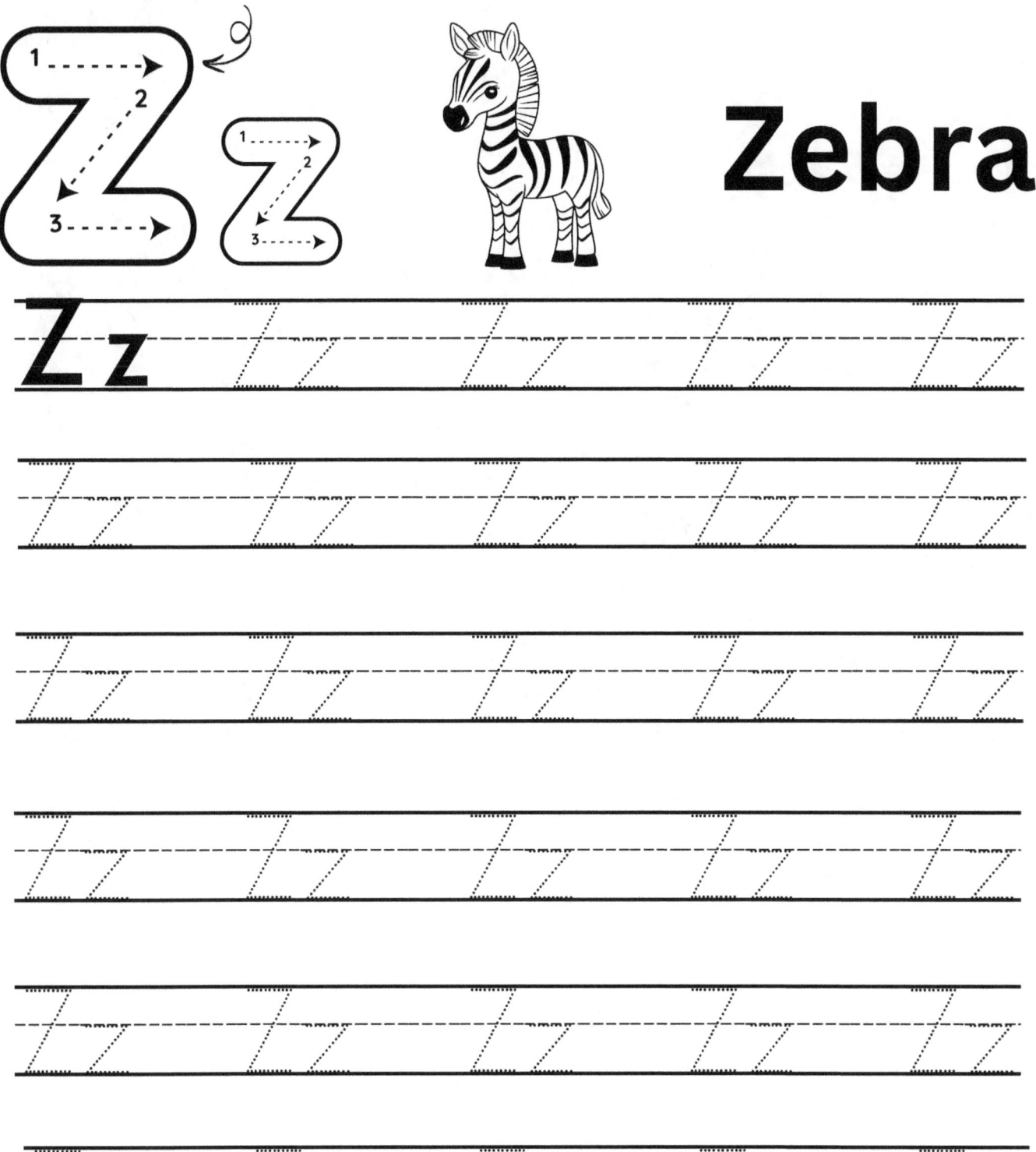

Zebra

NOTES

NOTES

NOTES

CERTIFICATE OF COMPLETION

This certificate is granted to

For completing

LEARN TO WRITE

Fun and Engaging Letter Tracing A-Z

LEARN TO WRITE

Fun and Engaging Handwriting Practice

Check back often for new releases.

Ruell's Publishing

WORKBOOKS

www.ruellspublishing.com